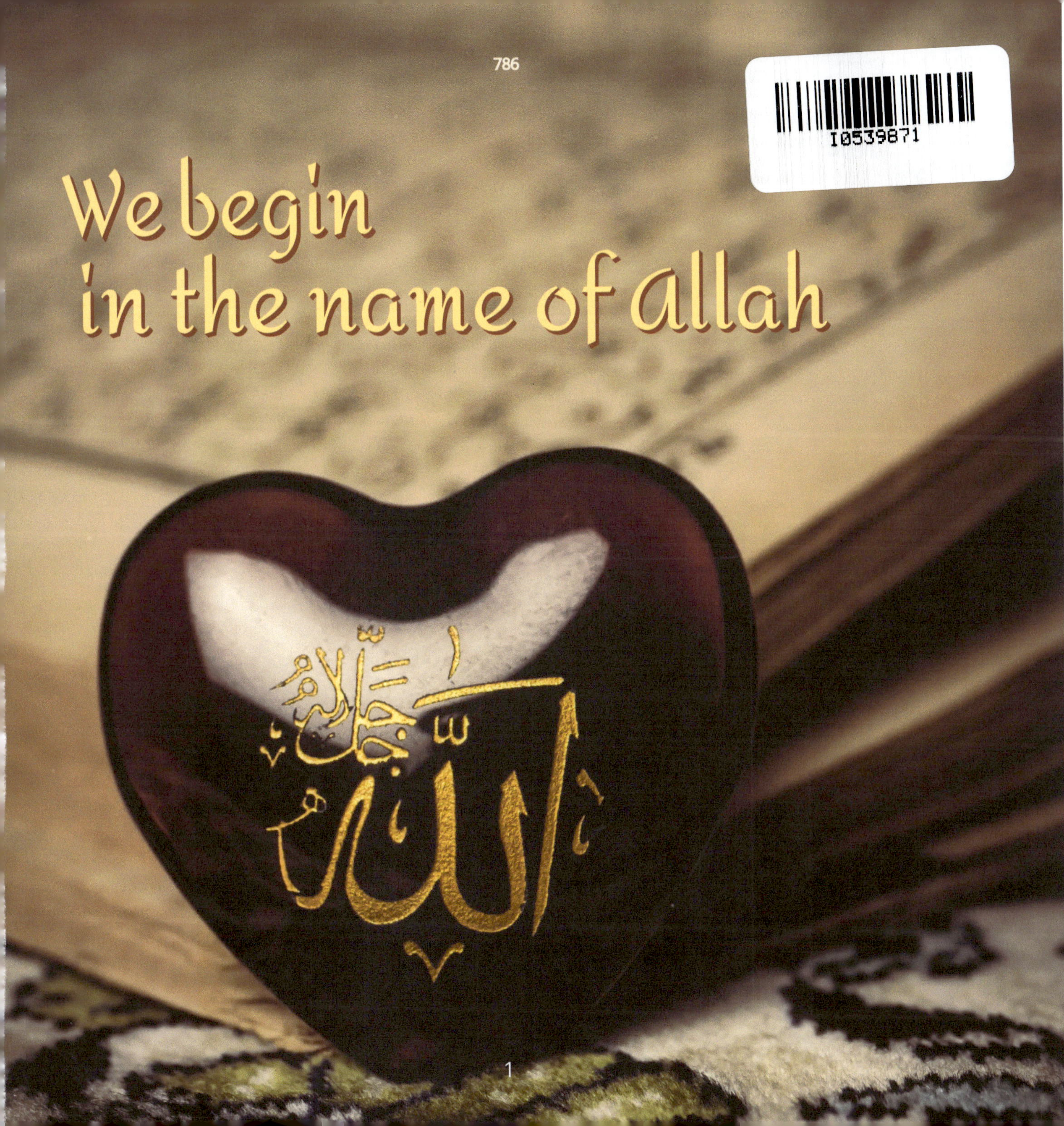
786
We begin
in the name of Allah
الله جل جلاله

Staten House

Disclaimer

The Quranic verses cited in this book are derived from widely available English translations for educational and informational purposes. These translations are provided to inspire reflection and understanding of the Quran's message but are not the author's own. Readers are encouraged to refer to the original Arabic text and consult reputable translations and scholars for deeper study.

The interpretations and discussions accompanying these verses reflect the author's understanding and are not intended to serve as authoritative religious rulings. Any errors or misunderstandings are unintended and are the sole responsibility of the author.

This book is designed to encourage intellectual and spiritual exploration and is not intended to promote or create religious conflict. The aim is to highlight the harmony between Quranic teachings and scientific understanding, fostering appreciation for the Quran's timeless wisdom.

This book is designed to inspire reflection on the Quran's messages and their relevance to the natural world, human development, and science. It is not intended to create or promote religious discord but rather to encourage intellectual and spiritual exploration.

Get your FREE gift and Volume 2 & 3 here:

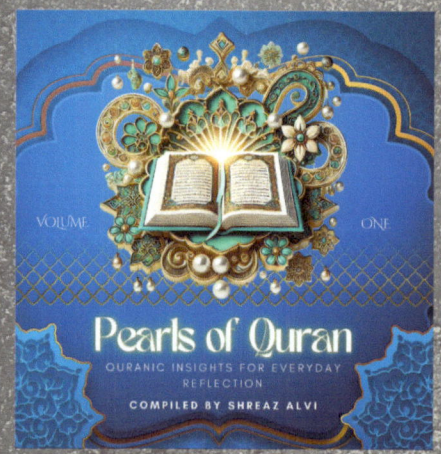

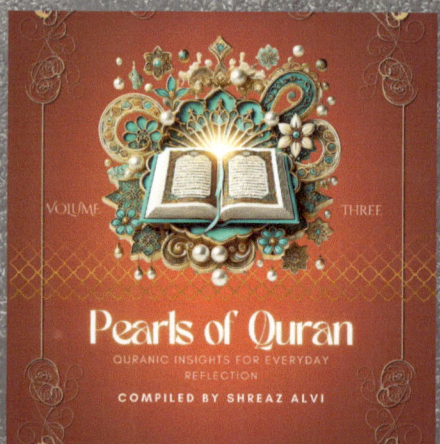

Is Quran the divine word?   -   Page 7

Love and Mercy   -   Page 19

Gratitude   -   Page 42

Patience   -   Page 65

Justice and Fairness   -   Page 88

Power of Prayer   -   Page 111

Dedicated to my Father

To the one who has been my unwavering guide in understanding the true essence of Islam and nurturing my connection to prayer. Dad your unwavering commitment to prayer has been a constant presence throughout my life. Thank you for being a living embodiment of faith, persistence, and inspiration.

Is the Quran the Divine Scripture from God?

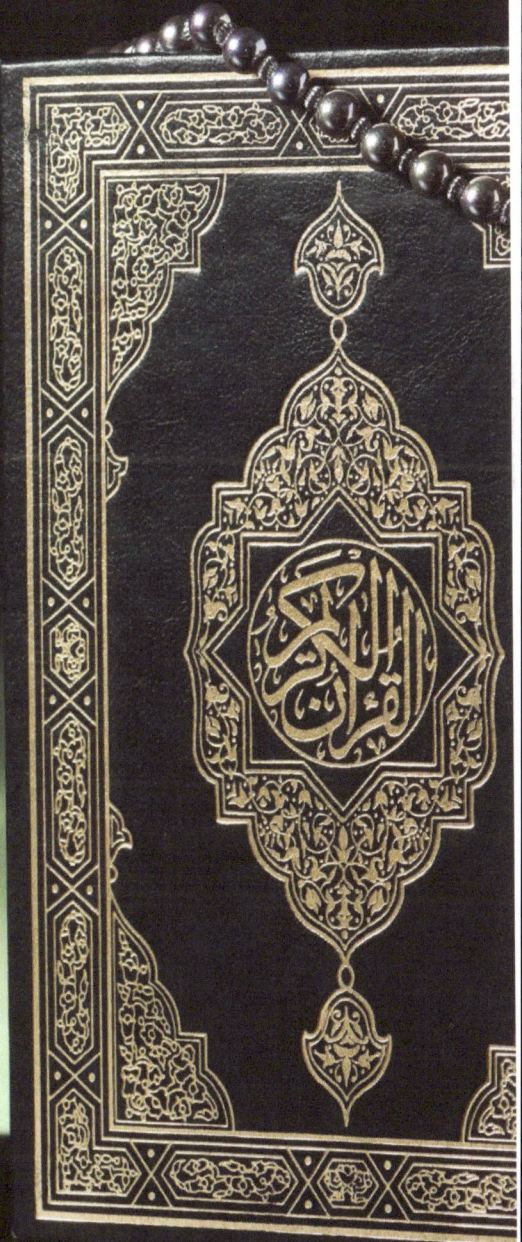

Is the Quran the Divine Scripture from God?

Muslims believe in monotheism, affirming that there is only One God, the Sovereign Creator of all things. They hold that everything in existence—whether the galaxies, the laws of nature, or even the process of evolution—is a manifestation of God's design. Muslims believe the same laws and balance that govern our Earth extend across the entire universe, harmonized with divine precision.

The Quran, revealed over 1,400 years ago, is regarded by Muslims as the exact and unaltered word of God. This claim is extraordinary, as it challenges readers to scrutinize its text for errors or contradictions, especially against the backdrop of modern scientific discoveries. What is remarkable is how the Quran aligns with phenomena uncovered centuries after its revelation. It is important to remember that Quran was revealed on Prophet Muhammad (pbuh) 1400 years ago and he did not know how to read or write. Keep this in mind as we go along and scrutinise this 1400 years old text that has preserved in single version over all this time.

Below are some examples, along with commentary to connect these verses to scientific findings:

Preservation of the Quran and the Life of the Prophet Muhammad

The Quran's Unchanging Text:
The Quran exists in one transcript worldwide, in its original Arabic. This has been verified by ancient manuscripts, such as the Birmingham Quran Manuscript, which dates back to the time of the Prophet Muhammad (peace be upon him). Its consistency over centuries stands unmatched.

"Indeed, it is We who sent down the Quran, and indeed, We will be its guardian." (Quran 15:9)
Commentary: This verse reflects the preservation of the Quran, a claim upheld by historical evidence.

The Prophet's Illiteracy:
Prophet Muhammad (peace be upon him) could neither read nor write, yet he delivered a scripture of unparalleled linguistic beauty. This fact underscores the Quran's divine origin.

"And you did not recite any scripture before it, nor did you write it with your hand. Otherwise, the falsifiers would have doubted." (Quran 29:48)
Commentary: Despite being illiterate, the Prophet conveyed the Quran's eloquence and depth, astonishing scholars and critics alike.

Scientific Signs in the Quran

The Expanding Universe:

Modern science confirmed the universe's expansion in 1929 when Edwin Hubble observed galaxies moving apart. The Quran alluded to this over a millennium earlier:

"And it is We who have built the universe with [Our creative] power; and verily, it is We who are steadily expanding it." (Quran 51:47)
Commentary: This verse aligns with the scientific discovery that the universe is continuously stretching, a concept unknown at the time.

The Big Bang and Life from Water:

The Quran describes the origin of the universe and the essential role of water in creating life, facts confirmed by the Big Bang theory (1927) and biology (19th century).

"Have those who disbelieve not considered that the heavens and the earth were a joined entity, and We separated them? And We made from water every living thing. Then will they not believe?" (Quran 21:30)

Commentary: The Quran's description of the heavens and Earth beginning as a single entity reflects modern cosmology.

Earth's Layers:

Geologists identified Earth's layers in the 19th century, long after the Quran referred to them.

"It is Allah who created seven heavens and of the earth, the like of them." (Quran 65:12)

Commentary: This verse speaks of the Earth's structure, mirroring the scientific discovery of its distinct layers.

Embryology:

The Quran describes the stages of human development in the womb with remarkable accuracy, which modern embryology confirmed in the 20th century.

"We created man from a drop of fluid, then made it into a clinging clot, then into a lump, then We formed bones, then clothed the bones with flesh." (Quran 23:13-14)

Commentary: These stages correspond precisely to the sequence observed in embryological development.

Pairs in Creation:

The Quran highlights the existence of pairs in all forms of creation, from plants to subatomic particles.

"Glory be to Him who created all pairs: of what the earth produces, of their own selves, and of what they do not know." (Quran 36:36)
Commentary: This verse anticipated discoveries about plant reproduction (17th century) and matter-antimatter pairs in quantum physics (20th century).

Orbits of Celestial Bodies:

The motion of celestial bodies, discovered in the 16th century, is described in the Quran with striking clarity.

"It is He who created the night and the day and the sun and the moon; all [heavenly bodies] are swimming in an orbit." (Quran 21:33)
Commentary: This verse describes the orbits of the sun and moon, long before Copernicus and Kepler explained such motions.

Earth's Spherical Shape:

The Quran alludes to the Earth's shape as a sphere, confirmed by scientists like Newton in the 17th century.

"And after that, He spread the earth." (Quran 79:30)
Commentary: The Arabic word dahaha (to spread or shape like an egg) hints at Earth's oblate spheroid form.

Iron "Sent Down" to Earth:

Modern science confirmed that iron on Earth originated from supernovae, as temperatures in the solar system are insufficient to produce heavy elements like iron.

"And We sent down iron, in which there is great strength and benefits for mankind." (Quran 57:25)
Commentary: This verse aligns with the 20th-century discovery that iron came from the remnants of stars.

Divisibility of Atoms:

The Quran states that even the smallest particle can be further divided, a fact only discovered in 1897 when J.J. Thomson identified the electron.

"Not an atom's weight in the heavens or the earth escapes Him, nor anything smaller or larger." (Quran 34:3)
Commentary: This verse reflects the modern understanding of atomic divisibility.

The Protective Atmosphere

The Quran describes the atmosphere's protective role, a concept scientifically confirmed in the 20th century.

"And We made the sky a protected ceiling, but they, from its signs, are turning away." (Quran 21:32)
Scientific Discovery: The Earth's atmosphere protects life by blocking harmful radiation from the Sun and preventing meteoroids from reaching the surface. This was understood with advancements in atmospheric science in the 20th century.
Reference: NASA on Earth's Atmosphere.

Commentary: The verse highlights the atmosphere's protective function, unknown during the 7th century.

Mountains as Stabilizers

The Quran describes mountains as stabilizers for the Earth, a concept confirmed by geologists in the 20th century.

"And He has set firm mountains in the earth so that it would not shake with you, and rivers and roads, so that you may be guided." (Quran 16:15)

Scientific Discovery: Modern geology confirms that mountains have deep roots that stabilize tectonic plates, preventing excessive movement. This concept was articulated in the 20th century.

Reference: USGS on Plate Tectonics.

Commentary: The verse aligns with the role of mountains as described in modern geological studies.

The Role of the Sun's Light

The Quran distinguishes between the Sun's light and the Moon's reflected light, a distinction only scientifically confirmed in modern times.

"It is He who made the Sun a shining light and the Moon a derived light and determined for it phases—that you may know the number of years and account [of time]." (Quran 10:5)

Scientific Discovery: The Sun emits its own light through nuclear fusion, while the Moon reflects sunlight. This was first understood in the 16th century through advancements in astronomy.

Reference: NASA on the Sun and Moon.

Commentary: The Quran's language precisely describes the Sun as a source of light and the Moon as reflecting it.

The Origin of the Universe as Smoke and Sound Waves

The Quran uniquely describes the origin of the universe as "smoke" and mentions God speaking to the heavens and Earth, commanding them to come into existence. This aligns with the scientific understanding of the early universe and the role of sound waves.

"Then He directed Himself to the heaven while it was smoke and said to it and to the earth, 'Come [into being], willingly or by compulsion.' They said, 'We have come willingly.'" (Quran 41:11)

Scientific Discovery: The early universe resembled a dense, hot gaseous state—akin to smoke. Moreover, quantum physics and cosmology have shown that sound waves generated during the Big Bang helped shape the distribution of matter in the universe, leading to its continuous expansion. These waves, known as "acoustic oscillations," were detected in cosmic microwave background radiation.

Reference: NASA on Cosmic Sound Waves.

Commentary: This verse remarkably describes both the gaseous state of the early universe and the role of sound (God's command) in initiating its formation and expansion.

The Quran uniquely mentions God "speaking" to the heavens and Earth during their formation, which aligns with the role sound waves played in shaping the universe's early structure. While this concept was scientifically confirmed through advanced studies of the cosmic microwave background radiation in the late 20th century, the Quran hinted at this reality over 1,400 years ago.

Together with the verse about the universe's expansion (Quran 51:47), these references demonstrate the Quran's remarkable alignment with modern cosmological discoveries. Such insights invite deep reflection and exploration, as the Quran itself urges:

"We will show them Our signs in the horizons and within themselves until it becomes clear to them that it is the truth." (Quran 41:53)

Deep Oceans and Internal Waves

The Quran describes the existence of darkness in deep oceans, a phenomenon confirmed with advancements in oceanography.

"Or [they are] like darknesses within an unfathomable sea which is covered by waves, upon which are waves, over which are clouds—darknesses, some of them upon others. If a man stretches out his hand, he can hardly see it." (Quran 24:40)

Scientific Discovery: The ocean's depths are pitch dark, as sunlight cannot penetrate beyond 1,000 meters. Subsurface waves, discovered in the 20th century, also occur at this depth.

The Water Cycle

The Quran accurately describes the water cycle, a process understood only in the 16th century.

"And We sent down rain from the sky in a measured amount and settled it in the earth. And indeed, We are able to take it away." (Quran 23:18)
"Do you not see that Allah drives clouds, then He brings them together, then He makes them into a mass, and you see the rain emerge from within them?" (Quran 24:43)

Scientific Discovery: The water cycle, involving evaporation, condensation, and precipitation, was not fully understood until Bernard Palissy's work in the 16th century.
Reference: National Geographic on the Water Cycle.

The Weight of Clouds

The Quran mentions the weight of clouds, a fact confirmed with modern meteorological tools.

"It is He who sends down rain from the sky, and He knows what is in the wombs. And no soul perceives what it will earn tomorrow, and no soul perceives in what land it will die. Indeed, Allah is Knowing and Acquainted." (Quran 31:34)

Scientific Discovery: Meteorologists estimate that clouds can weigh millions of tons, depending on their density and size.
Reference: NOAA on Cloud Weight.
Commentary: The Quran highlights the massive weight of clouds, a fact that became measurable only with modern meteorology.

The Function of Fingerprints

The Quran hints at the uniqueness of human fingerprints, a fact scientifically discovered in the 19th century.

"Does man think that We will not assemble his bones? Yes. [We are] able [even] to proportion his fingertips." (Quran 75:3-4)

Scientific Discovery: Sir Francis Galton discovered the uniqueness of fingerprints in 1880, which became foundational to forensic science.
Reference: NIH on Fingerprint Science.
Commentary: The verse emphasizes the intricate design of fingertips, now known to be unique identifiers.

The Barrier Between Saltwater and Freshwater

The Quran describes a barrier between saltwater and freshwater, a phenomenon confirmed by oceanography in the 20th century.

"He released the two seas, meeting [side by side]; between them is a barrier [so] neither of them transgresses." (Quran 55:19-20)

Scientific Discovery: This phenomenon, known as the halocline, describes the meeting of freshwater and saltwater bodies without mixing, often observed in estuaries. Jacques Cousteau documented this in the 1960s.
Reference: Woods Hole Oceanographic Institution.
Commentary: This verse captures the scientific reality of water stratification.

Conclusion: An Invitation to Reflect

The Quran continues to inspire reflection and exploration, harmonizing faith and reason. Its verses challenge humanity to seek knowledge and connect with the Creator through an understanding of the natural world.

As the Quran states:
"Indeed, in the creation of the heavens and the earth, and the alternation of the night and the day, are signs for those of understanding." (Quran 3:190)

May these signs guide you in seeking the truth and discovering the beauty of the Quran's message. May God bless you with wisdom and peace. Amen.

The Quran's message is universal. It speaks to the soul, offering lessons on love, mercy, patience, gratitude, justice, and the wonders of creation. Whether you are a believer seeking deeper understanding or someone curious about the Quran's teachings, this book is designed to create moments of connection and contemplation.

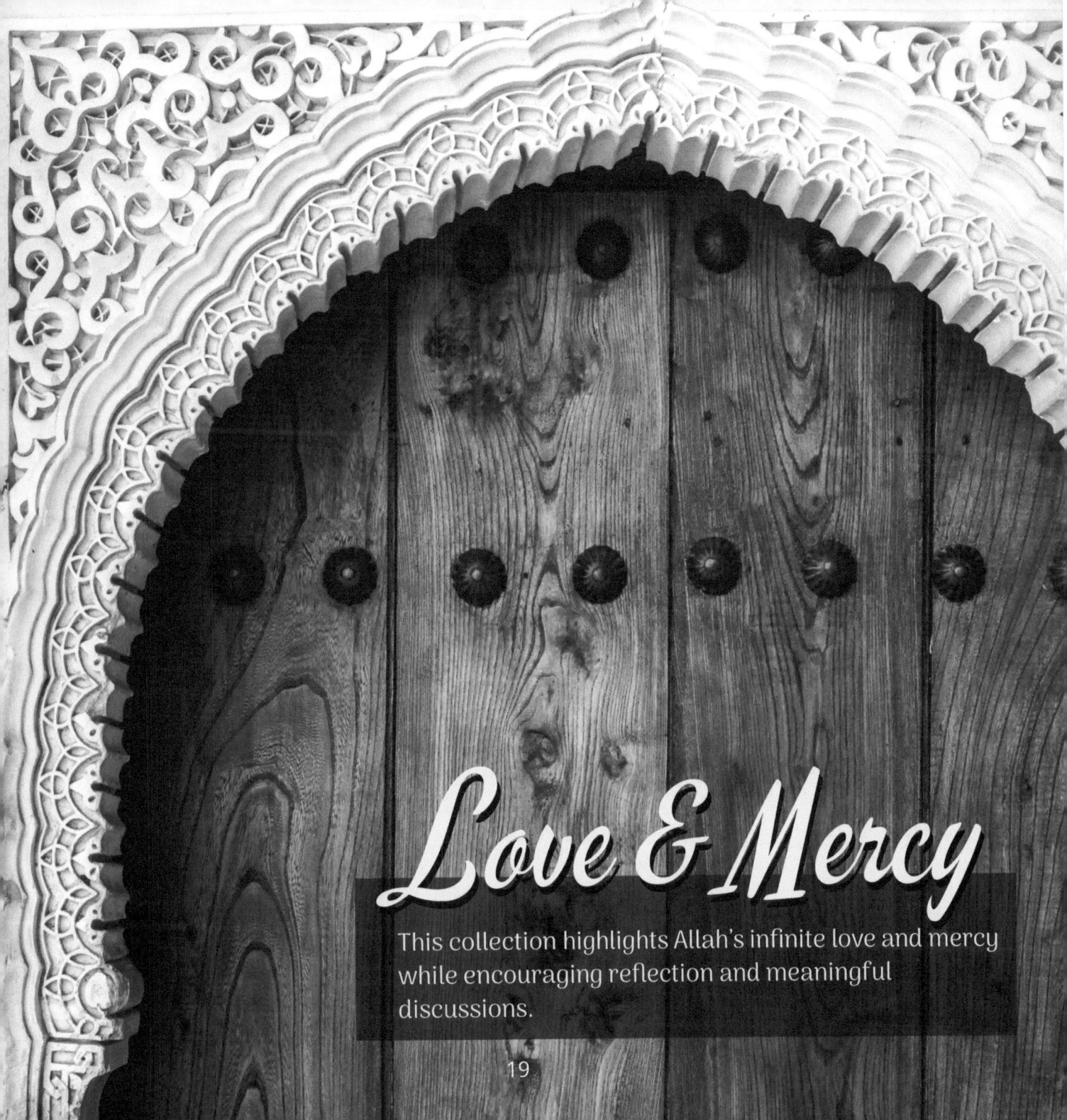

Love & Mercy

This collection highlights Allah's infinite love and mercy while encouraging reflection and meaningful discussions.

19

1. Surah Al-Buruj (85:14)
"And He is the Most Forgiving, the Most Loving."

Reflection:
Allah's love and forgiveness are boundless, far surpassing human capacity. His attribute of being "The Most Loving" reminds us that we are always cared for, no matter our mistakes.

Ponder:
How does knowing Allah's love and forgiveness affect the way you treat yourself and others?

2. Surah Al-A'raf (7:156)
"Indeed, My Mercy encompasses all things."

Reflection:
This verse reminds us that Allah's mercy is infinite and all-encompassing, covering every part of our lives and existence.

Prompt:
Can you recall a moment in your life when you felt Allah's mercy in an unexpected way?

3. Surah Aal-E-Imran (3:31)

"Say, 'If you should love Allah, then follow me, so Allah will love you and forgive your sins.'"

Reflection:

Loving Allah is intertwined with following His guidance. This love brings immense blessings, including forgiveness and spiritual growth.

Prompt:

How can following the Prophet Muhammad (peace be upon him) help deepen your connection with Allah?

4. Surah Aal-E-Imran (3:159)

"Indeed, Allah loves those who rely upon Him."

Reflection:

Trusting Allah, especially during hardships, is a sign of faith and a pathway to His love.

Prompt:

How can you practice reliance on Allah in your daily challenges?

5. Surah Aal-E-Imran (3:134)
"And Allah loves the doers of good."

Reflection:

Acts of kindness and goodness are highly valued in Islam. Being a source of goodness not only benefits others but also strengthens your relationship with Allah.

Prompt:

Share a moment when doing good brought you closer to Allah or someone else.

6. Surah An-Nisa (4:96)
"And Allah is ever Forgiving and Merciful."

Reflection:
Allah's forgiveness is constant, reminding us to never lose hope in His mercy, regardless of our shortcomings.

Prompt: How can this verse inspire you to forgive others and yourself?

7. Surah Ta-Ha (20:82)

"But indeed, I am the Perpetual Forgiver of whoever repents and believes and does righteousness and then continues in guidance."

Reflection: Allah's forgiveness is always available for those who sincerely seek it. His mercy opens doors to redemption and personal growth.

Prompt: How does this verse motivate you to seek forgiveness and stay on the right path?

8. Surah Az-Zumar (39:53)
"Do not despair of the mercy of Allah. Indeed, Allah forgives all sins."

Reflection: This verse offers hope and comfort, assuring us that no sin is too great for Allah's mercy.

Prompt: How can this verse help someone who feels distant from Allah because of their mistakes?

9. Surah An-Nur (24:22)

"Let them pardon and overlook. Would you not like that Allah should forgive you?"

Reflection: Forgiving others is a pathway to receiving Allah's forgiveness and mercy.

Prompt: How can practicing forgiveness improve your relationships and spiritual well-being?

10. Surah Al-Anfal (8:2)

"The believers are only those who, when Allah is mentioned, their hearts become fearful."

Reflection: This verse highlights the deep connection between love for Allah and a sense of awe and humility in His presence.

Prompt: How can cultivating this awe and humility help deepen your faith?

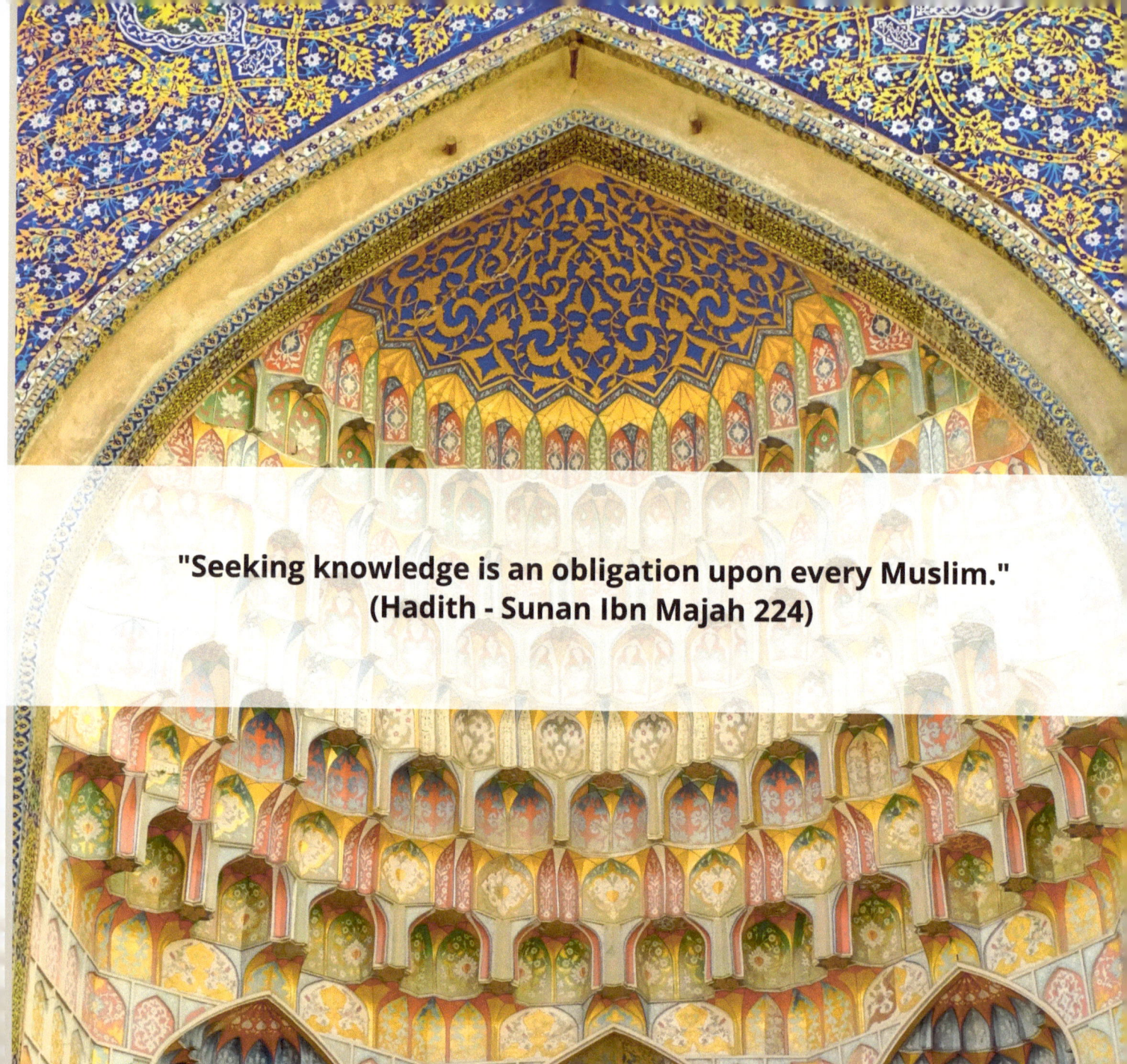

"Seeking knowledge is an obligation upon every Muslim."
(Hadith - Sunan Ibn Majah 224)

"He who follows a path in quest of knowledge,
Allah will make the path of Jannah easy for him."
(Hadith - Sahih Muslim 2699)

11. Surah Al-Baqarah (2:222)

"Indeed, Allah loves those who are constantly repentant and loves those who purify themselves."

Reflection: Repentance and purification are acts of humility and love toward Allah, showing our desire to grow spiritually.

Prompt: What steps can you take to make repentance and purification part of your daily routine?

12. Surah Al-Hadid (57:28)

"Fear Allah and believe in His Messenger; He will give you a double portion of His mercy."

Reflection: Allah's mercy multiplies for those who live with mindfulness and faith.

Prompt: How can living with greater mindfulness increase your sense of Allah's mercy?

13. Surah At-Tawbah (9:99)
"Allah will admit them to His mercy. Indeed, Allah is Forgiving and Merciful."

Reflection: This verse reassures us that Allah's mercy is a reward for faith and sincerity.

Prompt: How can you remind yourself of Allah's mercy during times of difficulty?

14. Surah Al-Furqan (25:70)

"Except for those who repent, believe, and do righteous work. For them Allah will replace their evil deeds with good."

Reflection: Allah's mercy not only forgives but also transforms our past into a source of growth and goodness.

Prompt: What does this verse teach us about the transformative power of repentance?

15. Surah Al-Isra (17:24)

"Lower to them the wing of humility out of mercy."

Reflection: Showing mercy and kindness, especially to parents, is an act of love that mirrors Allah's mercy.

Prompt: How can this verse inspire you to treat your loved ones with more compassion?

16. Surah Al-Baqarah (2:286)

"Allah does not burden a soul beyond that it can bear."

Reflection: Allah's love ensures that we are never given more than we can handle, even when we feel overwhelmed.

Prompt: How does this verse help you trust Allah during hardships?

17. Surah Al-An'am (6:54)
"Your Lord has decreed upon Himself mercy."

Reflection: Allah's mercy is not conditional; it is a promise He has made to His creation.

Prompt: How does this promise help you build trust in Allah's plans?

18. Surah An-Nahl (16:18)

"And if you should count the favors of Allah, you could not enumerate them."

Reflection: Allah's love is reflected in the countless blessings we enjoy every day, many of which we take for granted.

Prompt: How can reflecting on Allah's blessings help cultivate gratitude and love?

19. Surah Ash-Shura (42:28)

"And it is He who sends down the rain after they have despaired and spreads His mercy."

Reflection: Just as rain revives the earth, Allah's mercy revives our hearts and souls during difficult times.

Prompt: How has Allah's mercy brought you relief when you least expected it?

20. Surah Al-Anbiya (21:107)

"And We have not sent you, [O Muhammad], except as a mercy to the worlds."

Reflection: The life and teachings of Prophet Muhammad (peace be upon him) are a living example of Allah's infinite mercy.

Prompt: How can following the example of the Prophet (peace be upon him) help us embody mercy in our lives?

Gratitude

This selection of verses on gratitude offers a rich foundation for reflection and meaningful discussions.

1. Surah Ibrahim (14:7)

"If you are grateful, I will surely increase you [in favor]."

Reflection: Gratitude is directly tied to abundance. By appreciating what we have, we invite more blessings into our lives.

Prompt: What are three things you are grateful for today, and how can you express that gratitude?

2. Surah Al-Baqarah (2:152)

"So remember Me; I will remember you. And be grateful to Me and do not deny Me."

Reflection: Remembering Allah and expressing gratitude strengthens our bond with Him and keeps us mindful of His blessings.

Prompt: How can you incorporate remembering Allah into your daily routine?

3. Surah Al-Baqarah (2:172)

"Eat of the good things which We have provided for you and be grateful to Allah."

Reflection: Even in something as simple as eating, gratitude connects us to the Provider of all sustenance.

Prompt: How does being grateful for food and drink change your relationship with these blessings?

4. Surah Al-Ankabut (29:17)

"So seek provision from Allah, and worship Him, and be grateful to Him."

Reflection: Gratefulness is an act of worship that acknowledges Allah as the sole provider of all good.

Prompt: How does recognizing Allah as the provider inspire trust and gratitude in your life?

5. Surah Az-Zumar (39:66)

"Rather, worship Allah and be among the grateful."

Reflection: Gratitude is intertwined with worship, reflecting our acknowledgment of Allah's gifts.

Prompt: How can your worship become an act of gratitude?

6. Surah An-Nahl (16:18)
"And if you should count the favors of Allah, you could not enumerate them."

Reflection: This verse reminds us of the countless blessings we often overlook.

Prompt: What are some subtle blessings in your life that you often take for granted?

7. Surah Luqman (31:12)
"Be grateful to Allah. And whoever is grateful is grateful for himself."

Reflection: Gratitude benefits the giver as much as the receiver, fostering contentment and happiness.

Prompt: How does expressing gratitude improve your outlook on life?

8. Surah Al-Baqarah (2:243)
"Indeed, Allah is full of bounty to the people, but most of them are not grateful."

Reflection: Gratitude requires mindfulness; without it, we risk overlooking Allah's endless bounties.

Prompt: How can you remind yourself to remain grateful throughout the day?

9. Surah Al-Isra (17:24)
"Say, 'My Lord, enable me to be grateful for Your favor which You have bestowed upon me.'"

Reflection: Gratitude is a skill that can be nurtured through prayer and practice.

Prompt: How often do you ask Allah to help you cultivate gratitude?

10. Surah Al-Mulk (67:23)

"It is He who has made for you hearing, vision, and hearts; little are you grateful."

Reflection: Gratitude for our senses and abilities is an essential part of appreciating Allah's gifts.

Prompt: How can you show gratitude for the faculties of hearing, sight, and intellect in your daily life?

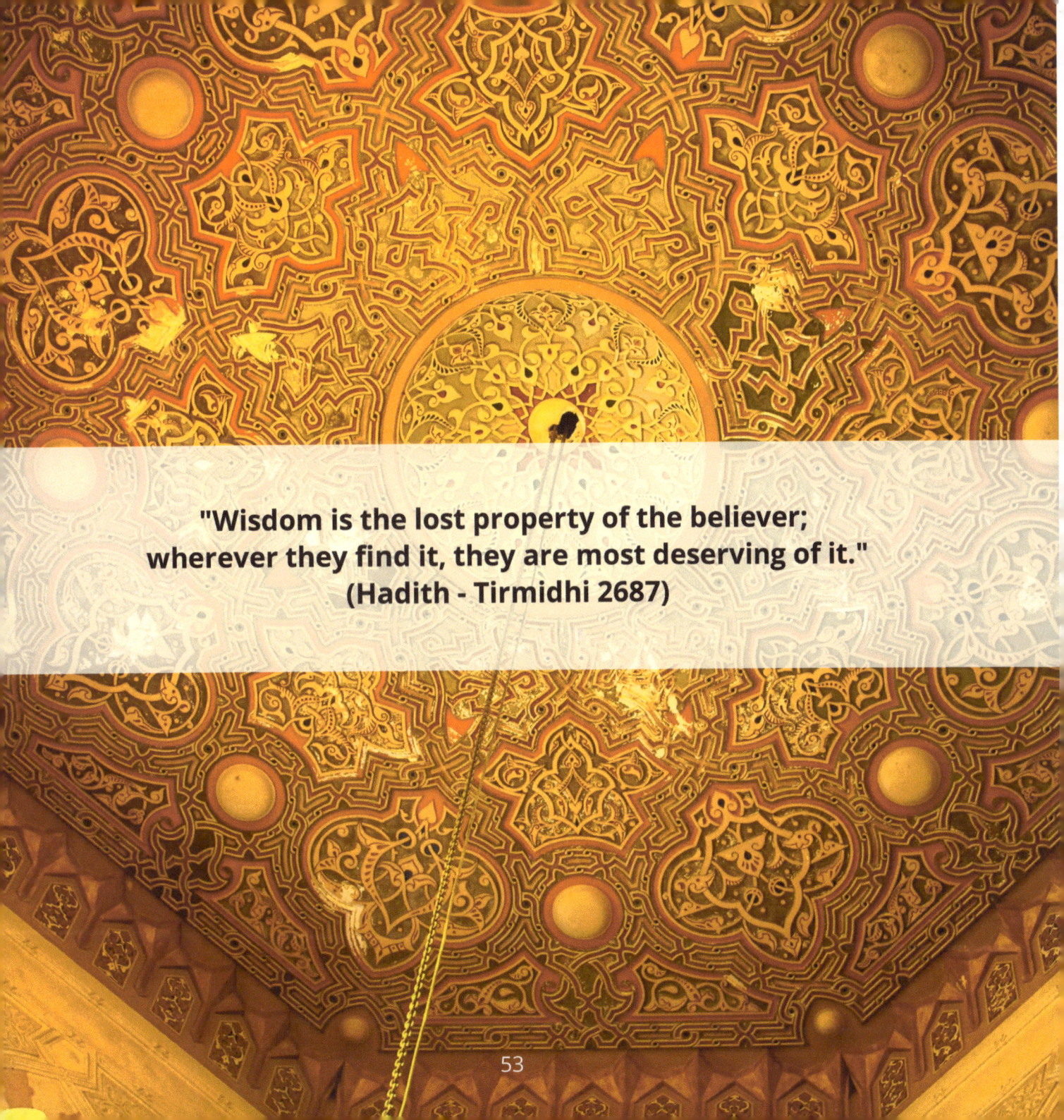

"Wisdom is the lost property of the believer;
wherever they find it, they are most deserving of it."
(Hadith - Tirmidhi 2687)

"The world is green and beautiful,
and Allah has appointed you His stewards over it."
(Hadith - Sahih Muslim 2742)

11. Surah Al-Insan (76:3)

"Indeed, We guided him to the way, be he grateful or be he ungrateful."

Reflection: Gratitude is a choice we make in response to Allah's guidance and blessings.

Prompt: What steps can you take to actively choose gratitude in challenging times?

12. Surah Al-Kahf (18:39)

"It was better for you to say, when you entered your garden, 'This is what Allah has willed; there is no power except with Allah.'"

Reflection: Acknowledging Allah as the source of all good strengthens our gratitude and humility.

Prompt: How can you remind yourself to attribute your successes to Allah?

13. Surah An-Nahl (16:114)

"Then eat of what Allah has provided for you which is lawful and good. And be grateful for the favor of Allah."

Reflection: Halal provisions are a direct blessing from Allah, deserving of our gratitude.

Prompt: How does being mindful of what you consume help you practice gratitude?

14. Surah Al-Baqarah (2:286)

"Allah does not burden a soul beyond that it can bear."

Reflection: Even challenges are a blessing, as they are tailored to our strength. Gratitude helps us find meaning in them.

Prompt: How can gratitude change your perspective on difficulties you face?

15. Surah Az-Zukhruf (43:13)

"Then exalt the name of your Lord when you mount upon it and say, 'Exalted is He who has subjected this to us.'"

Reflection: Gratitude extends to the tools and conveniences Allah has made available to us.

Prompt: How can you express gratitude for modern conveniences in your life?

16. Surah Ad-Duha (93:11)
"But as for the favor of your Lord, report it."

Reflection: Sharing Allah's blessings is an act of gratitude that spreads joy and inspires others.

Prompt: What is one blessing you can share with someone else today?

17. Surah Al-Baqarah (2:185)

"Allah intends for you ease and does not intend for you hardship, and [He wants] for you to complete the period and to glorify Allah for that [to] which He has guided you and perhaps you will be grateful."

Reflection: Even acts of worship like fasting are designed to nurture ease and gratitude in our lives.

Prompt: How has Ramadan or fasting helped you appreciate Allah's blessings?

18. Surah Yunus (10:12)

"And when affliction touches man, he calls upon Us, whether lying on his side or sitting or standing. But when We remove his affliction, he continues [in disobedience]."

Reflection: Gratitude in times of ease is as important as supplication in times of difficulty.

Prompt: How can you ensure that your gratitude remains constant, whether in hardship or ease?

19. Surah An-Nisa (4:147)
"What would Allah do with your punishment if you are grateful and believe?"

Reflection: Gratitude and faith are shields from Allah's displeasure and pathways to His mercy.

Prompt: How does your gratitude reflect your faith in Allah?

20. Surah An-Nahl (16:97)

"Whoever does righteousness, whether male or female, while he is a believer - We will surely cause him to live a good life."

Reflection: Gratitude leads to righteousness, which in turn brings contentment and a fulfilling life.

Prompt: How can gratitude motivate you to perform more acts of righteousness?

Patience

This section highlights the Quran's profound teachings on patience and perseverance, offering practical lessons and prompts for reflection.

1. Surah Al-Baqarah (2:153)
"Indeed, Allah is with the patient."

Reflection: This verse reassures us that patience brings divine companionship, providing strength and comfort in difficult times.

Prompt: Can you share a moment when your patience led to a positive outcome or spiritual growth?

2. Surah Al-Baqarah (2:155)

"And We will surely test you with something of fear and hunger and a loss of wealth and lives and fruits, but give good tidings to the patient."

Reflection: Life's trials are opportunities for spiritual refinement, and patience is the key to navigating them successfully.

Prompt: How does this verse inspire you to view challenges as opportunities for growth?

3. Surah Al-Baqarah (2:45)
"And seek help through patience and prayer."

Reflection: Patience and prayer go hand in hand as tools to overcome difficulties and strengthen our connection with Allah.

Prompt: How can you incorporate patience and prayer into your daily routine to face life's challenges?

4. Surah Az-Zumar (39:10)
"Indeed, the patient will be given their reward without account."

Reflection: The reward for patience is limitless, reflecting its immense value in Allah's eyes.

Prompt: What are some ways you can cultivate patience in moments of frustration?

5. Surah An-Nahl (16:96)

"And We will surely give those who were patient their reward according to the best of what they used to do."

Reflection: Patience magnifies the value of good deeds, earning immense reward from Allah.

Prompt: How does this verse encourage you to persevere in doing good, even when it's difficult?

6. Surah Ash-Shura (42:43)
"And whoever is patient and forgives - indeed, that is of the matters [requiring] determination."

Reflection: Patience coupled with forgiveness is a noble trait that requires strength and resolve.

Prompt: How can practicing forgiveness alongside patience improve your relationships?

7. Surah Al-Baqarah (2:177)
"Patience in poverty and hardship and during battle. Those are the ones who have been true."

Reflection: True faith is demonstrated through patience, especially in challenging circumstances.

Prompt: How do you stay true to your values when faced with adversity?

8. Surah Al-Anfal (8:46)

"Be patient. Indeed, Allah is with the patient."

Reflection: Repeated reminders of Allah's support for the patient reinforce the importance of steadfastness in faith.

Prompt: How can this promise motivate you to remain patient during difficult times?

9. Surah Maryam (19:65)
"So rely upon Him and have patience in His obedience."

Reflection: Patience in maintaining devotion and reliance on Allah is a mark of true submission.

Prompt: What practices help you stay patient in your spiritual journey?

10. Surah Al-Imran (3:200)
"O you who have believed, persevere and endure and remain stationed and fear Allah that you may be successful."

Reflection: Success in faith requires perseverance, endurance, and mindfulness of Allah.

Prompt: How can you apply this verse to build resilience in your personal life?

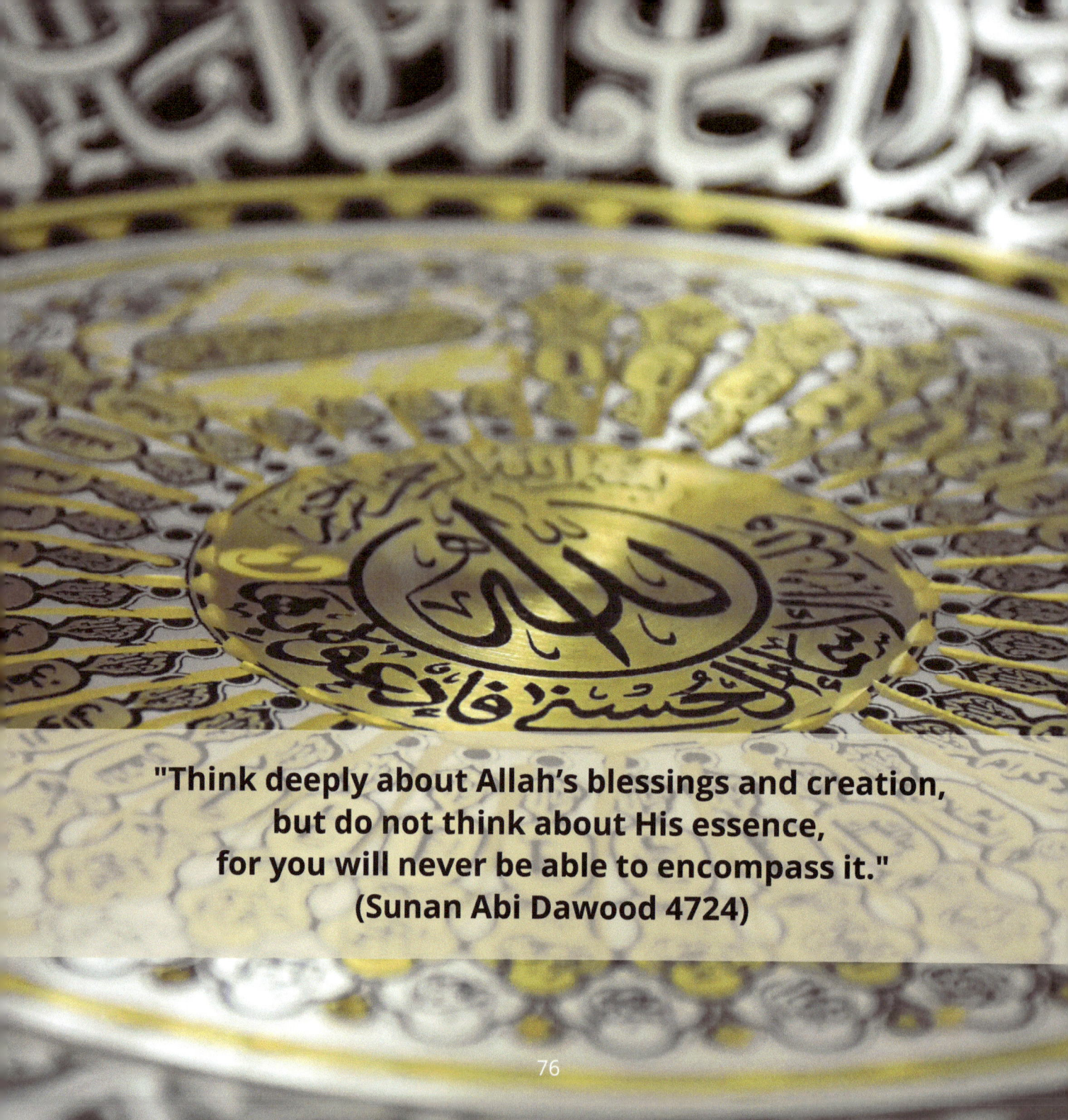

"Think deeply about Allah's blessings and creation,
but do not think about His essence,
for you will never be able to encompass it."
(Sunan Abi Dawood 4724)

"The best among you are those who learn the Quran and teach it."
(Sahih al-Bukhari 5027)

11. Surah Al-Ankabut (29:69)
"And those who strive for Us - We will surely guide them to Our ways."

Reflection: Patience and effort in seeking Allah's guidance lead to success in both this life and the hereafter.

Prompt: How can you increase your efforts to seek Allah's guidance in daily life?

12. Surah Yusuf (12:18)
"So patience is most fitting."

Reflection: This simple yet profound statement emphasizes the beauty and necessity of patience in times of distress.

Prompt: How can you remind yourself to practice patience when faced with sudden challenges?

13. Surah At-Tur (52:48)
"And be patient for the decision of your Lord, for indeed, you are in Our eyes."

Reflection: Knowing that Allah is watching over you makes patience easier during life's trials.

Prompt: How can you find comfort in Allah's care during uncertain times?

14. Surah Taha (20:130)
"So be patient over what they say and exalt [Allah] with praise."

Reflection: Patience in the face of criticism or adversity is a sign of inner strength and faith.

Prompt: How can you turn to gratitude and praise during moments of difficulty?

15. Surah As-Saffat (37:102)

"O my son, indeed I have seen in a dream that I [must] sacrifice you, so see what you think."

Reflection: This verse highlights Prophet Ibrahim's (AS) patience and submission to Allah's command, demonstrating ultimate faith.

Prompt: How does this example inspire you to trust Allah's plans?

16. Surah Al-Ahqaf (46:35)
"So be patient, as were those of determination among the messengers."

Reflection: The patience of the prophets serves as a model for believers to emulate.

Prompt: How can reflecting on the lives of the prophets strengthen your own patience?

17. Surah Al-Baqarah (2:286)
"Allah does not burden a soul beyond that it can bear."

Reflection: This verse reassures us that every challenge is within our capacity to endure.

Prompt: How does this verse help you remain patient when faced with hardships?

18. Surah Hud (11:11)

"Except for those who are patient and do righteous deeds; those will have forgiveness and great reward."

Reflection: Patience combined with righteous actions earns both forgiveness and immense reward from Allah.

Prompt: How can you use this verse as motivation to pair patience with good deeds?

19. Surah Al-Muzzammil (73:10)
"And be patient over what they say and avoid them with gracious avoidance."

Reflection: This verse emphasizes patience in dealing with criticism and negativity with dignity.

Prompt: How can you practice "gracious avoidance" in challenging interpersonal situations?

20. Surah Al-Ahqaf (46:15)

"We have enjoined upon man to be dutiful to his parents... and to say, 'My Lord, enable me to be grateful and patient.'"

Reflection: Patience and gratitude are essential in fulfilling the duties Allah has set upon us, including honoring our parents.

Prompt: How can you show patience and gratitude in your relationships with loved ones?

Justice and Fairness

This collection highlights the Quran's profound emphasis on justice as a foundation for individual and societal harmony.

1. Surah An-Nisa (4:135)

"O you who have believed, be persistently standing firm in justice, witnesses for Allah, even if it be against yourselves or parents and relatives."

Reflection: Justice requires impartiality, even when it's difficult or against one's own interests. This verse emphasizes Allah's high regard for fairness.

Prompt: How can this verse guide us in making unbiased decisions in our daily lives?

2. Surah Al-Ma'idah (5:8)

"Do not let the hatred of a people prevent you from being just. Be just; that is nearer to righteousness."

Reflection: Justice must be upheld even toward those we dislike, as it is a key element of righteousness.

Prompt: How can you practice fairness when dealing with those who may have wronged you?

3. Surah An-Nahl (16:90)

"Indeed, Allah commands you to uphold justice and to do good and to give to relatives."

Reflection: This verse ties justice to goodness and generosity, making it a cornerstone of social harmony.

Prompt: How can justice and kindness work together to create stronger communities?

4. Surah Al-Baqarah (2:282)

"And let not the scribe refuse to write as Allah has taught him. So let him write and let the one who has the obligation dictate with justice."

Reflection: Justice in agreements ensures accountability and fairness in financial and personal dealings.

Prompt: How does this verse emphasize the importance of fairness in contracts and commitments?

5. Surah Al-Mumtahanah (60:8)

"Allah does not forbid you from being righteous and just toward those who have not fought you."

Reflection: Justice extends even to those who are not part of one's faith or community, promoting universal fairness.

Prompt: How can this verse inspire fairness and kindness in interfaith or intercultural relationships?

6. Surah Al-Baqarah (2:188)

"And do not consume one another's wealth unjustly or send it [in bribery] to the rulers."

Reflection: Economic justice is a crucial aspect of societal well-being, and corruption undermines fairness.

Prompt: How can this verse shape ethical financial practices in both personal and professional life?

7. Surah Al-An'am (6:152)

"And do not approach the orphan's property except in a way that is best until he reaches maturity."

Reflection: Protecting the vulnerable, especially orphans, is a critical part of maintaining justice in society.

Prompt: How can we apply this principle to advocate for the rights of vulnerable populations today?

8. Surah An-Nisa (4:58)

"Indeed, Allah commands you to render trusts to whom they are due and when you judge between people to judge with justice."

Reflection: Fulfilling trusts and judging fairly are divine commands that foster trust and societal order.

Prompt: How can we ensure that we fulfill our responsibilities with integrity?

9. Surah Hud (11:85)

"And do not deprive people of their due and do not commit abuse on the earth, spreading corruption."

Reflection: Justice includes fairness in dealings and avoiding harm to others or the environment.

Prompt: How does this verse inspire ethical practices in trade and environmental stewardship?

10. Surah Al-Isra (17:35)

"And give full measure when you measure and weigh with an even balance."

Reflection: Justice in trade and commerce is emphasized as a sign of integrity and fairness.

Prompt: How can we practice fairness in our professional and personal transactions?

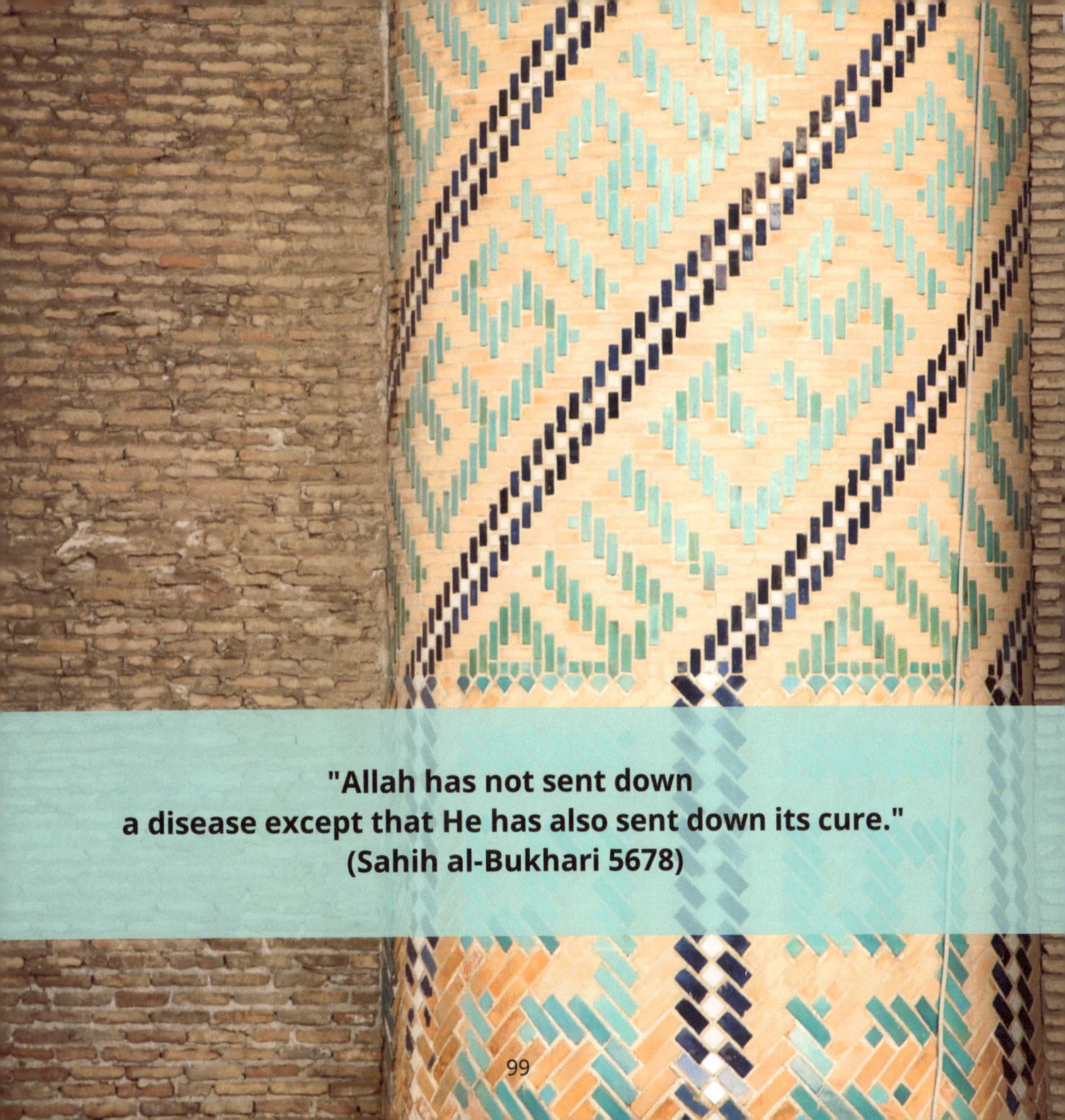

"Allah has not sent down
a disease except that He has also sent down its cure."
(Sahih al-Bukhari 5678)

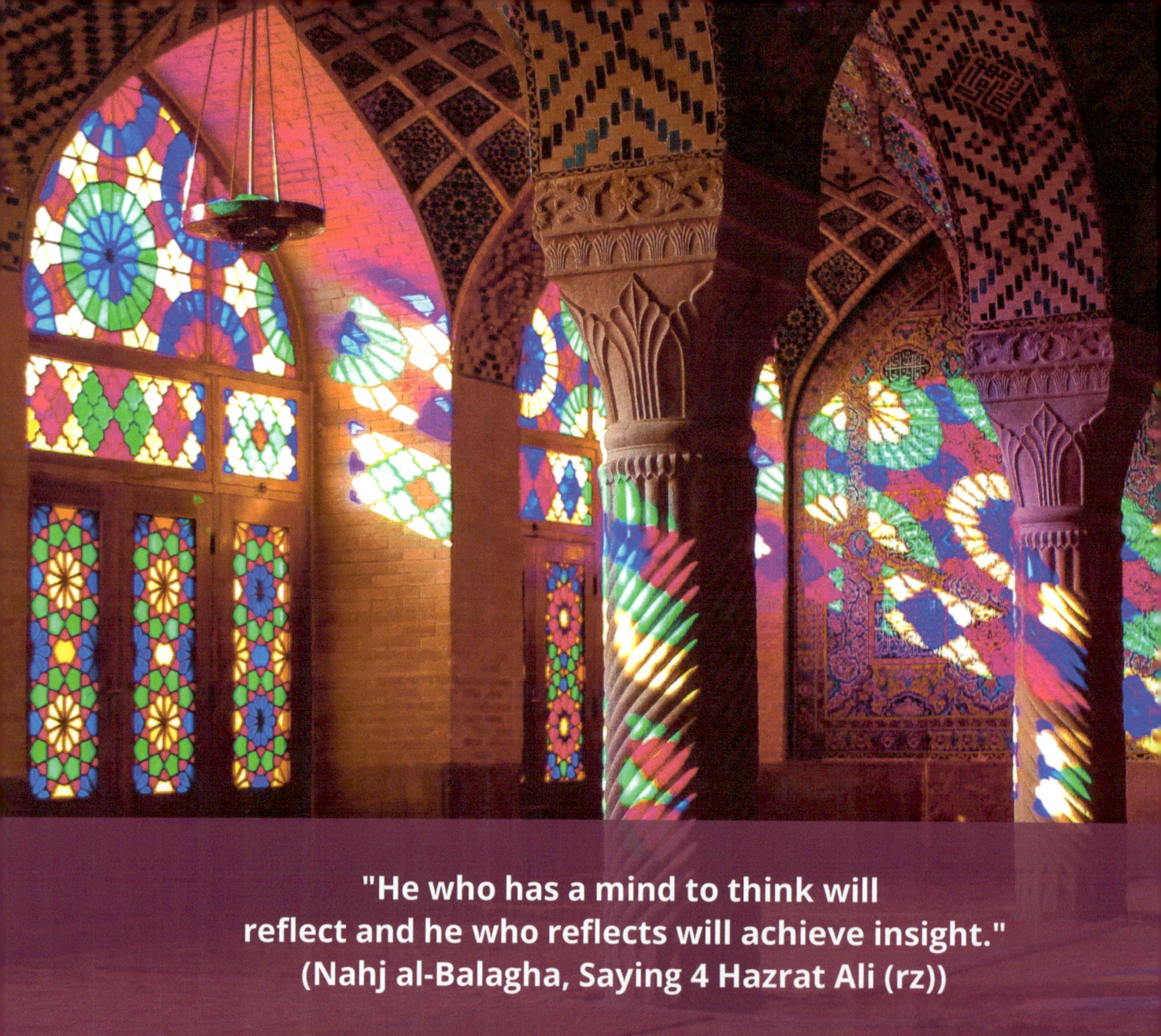

"He who has a mind to think will
reflect and he who reflects will achieve insight."
(Nahj al-Balagha, Saying 4 Hazrat Ali (rz))

11. Surah Ash-Shu'ara (26:183)

"And do not deprive people of their due and do not act wickedly on the earth, spreading corruption."

Reflection: This verse reiterates the importance of not exploiting others and preserving fairness in all actions.

Prompt: How can this verse encourage ethical leadership in communities?

12. Surah Al-Ma'idah (5:42)

"Indeed, Allah loves those who act justly."

Reflection: Justice is not just a duty but a quality beloved by Allah, highlighting its spiritual significance.

Prompt: How does knowing Allah loves justice inspire you to act fairly?

13. Surah Al-Hujurat (49:9)

"And if two factions among the believers should fight, then make settlement between the two. But if one of them oppresses the other, then fight against the one that oppresses."

Reflection: Justice includes standing up against oppression and working toward reconciliation.

Prompt: How can this verse guide us in resolving conflicts justly?

14. Surah At-Tawbah (9:71)

"The believing men and believing women are allies of one another. They enjoin what is right and forbid what is wrong."

Reflection: Justice is a collective responsibility, and believers are encouraged to uphold it together.

Prompt: How can communities work together to promote justice and fairness?

15. Surah Al-An'am (6:141)

"And give its due [zakah] on the day of its harvest, and do not spend wastefully."

Reflection: Justice includes financial responsibility, such as giving zakah and avoiding extravagance.

Prompt: How can practicing zakah and financial moderation promote social equity?

16. Surah Az-Zukhruf (43:32)

"Do they distribute the mercy of your Lord? It is We who have apportioned among them their livelihood."

Reflection: Justice includes accepting Allah's divine wisdom in distributing resources and blessings.

Prompt: How can this verse help us trust Allah's justice even in times of inequality?

17. Surah Al-Baqarah (2:279)

"If you do not, then be informed of a war [against you] from Allah and His Messenger. But if you repent, you may have your principal."

Reflection: Interest-based transactions exploit the vulnerable, and justice demands fairness in financial dealings.

Prompt: How can we ensure fairness and ethical practices in lending and borrowing?

18. Surah Al-Mumtahanah (60:1)

"You will not find a people who believe in Allah and the Last Day having affection for those who oppose Allah and His Messenger."

Reflection: Justice does not mean compromising one's values; it requires standing firm in truth while being fair.

Prompt: How can we balance fairness with staying true to our principles?

19. Surah Al-Hadid (57:25)

"And We sent with them the Scripture and the balance that the people may maintain [their affairs] in justice."

Reflection: The Quran itself is a guide for establishing justice, reflecting its central role in our lives.

Prompt: How does the Quran inspire you to act justly in your daily interactions?

20. Surah Al-Isra (17:26)

"And give the relative his right, and [also] the poor and the traveler, and do not spend wastefully."

Reflection: Justice includes caring for the needs of others, especially the less fortunate, without squandering resources.

Prompt: How can this verse inspire fairness and generosity in your community?

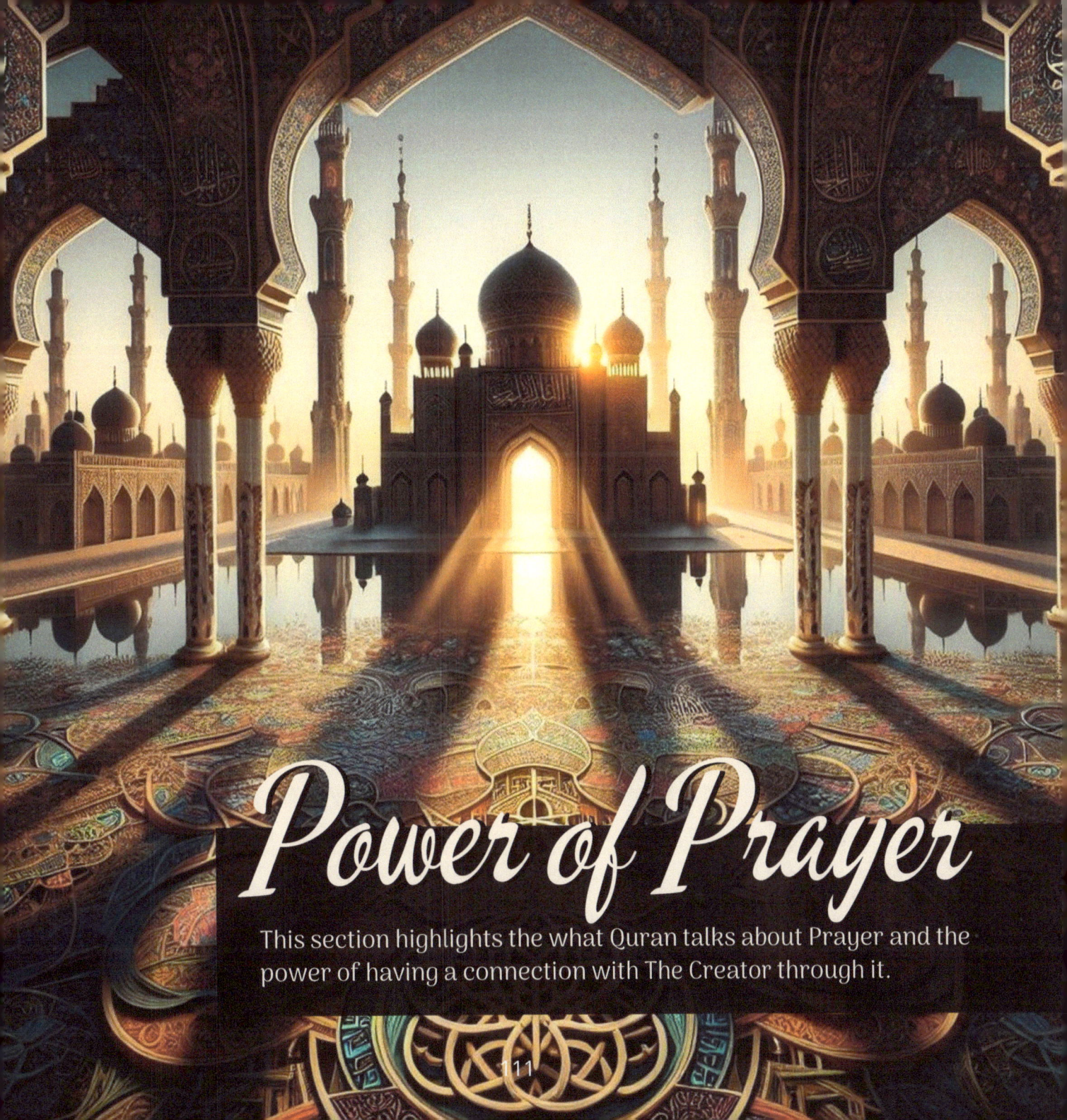

Power of Prayer

This section highlights the what Quran talks about Prayer and the power of having a connection with The Creator through it.

1. Surah Al-Baqarah (2:186)

"And when My servants ask you concerning Me, indeed I am near. I respond to the invocation of the supplicant when he calls upon Me."

Reflection: This verse reminds us of Allah's closeness and His readiness to respond to our prayers. It is a source of comfort and hope.

Prompt: How does knowing that Allah is always near encourage you to pray more often?

2. Surah Ghafir (40:60)
"Call upon Me; I will respond to you."

Reflection: Allah's promise to respond to our prayers is a profound invitation to turn to Him with sincerity and trust.

Prompt: How can this promise motivate you to rely on prayer during challenging times?

3. Surah Maryam (19:4)

"My Lord, indeed my bones have weakened, and my head has filled with white, and never have I been in my supplication to You, my Lord, unhappy."

Reflection: Prophet Zakariya (AS) exemplifies unwavering hope in prayer, regardless of his circumstances.

Prompt: How does this verse inspire you to remain hopeful in prayer, even when things seem difficult?

4. Surah Al-Anbiya (21:89)

"And [mention] Zechariah, when he called to his Lord, 'My Lord, do not leave me alone [without an heir], while You are the best of inheritors.'"

Reflection: This verse shows how prayer is not only a plea but also an acknowledgment of Allah's ultimate power.

Prompt: How does prayer help you surrender your desires to Allah's wisdom?

5. Surah Al-Baqarah (2:45)

"And seek help through patience and prayer."

Reflection: Prayer is a source of strength, providing spiritual support during hardships.

Prompt: How can you make prayer a habitual response in times of difficulty?

6. Surah Hud (11:88)

"And my success is not but through Allah. Upon Him I have relied, and to Him I return."

Reflection: Prayer is an act of reliance on Allah, acknowledging that success comes only through Him.

Prompt: How does reliance on prayer influence your sense of control in life?

7. Surah Al-Isra (17:110)

"Call upon Allah or call upon the Most Merciful. Whichever [name] you call - to Him belong the best names."

Reflection: Allah's many names reflect His attributes, encouraging us to call upon Him in every situation.

Prompt: How do Allah's names enhance the way you make your prayers?

8. Surah Ash-Shu'ara (26:62)
"Indeed, with me is my Lord; He will guide me."

Reflection: This verse shows the confidence and faith that prayer instills, especially in dire circumstances.

Prompt: How can prayer help you cultivate unwavering trust in Allah's guidance?

9. Surah Al-Muzzammil (73:20)

"And establish prayer and give zakah and loan Allah a goodly loan. And whatever good you put forward for yourselves – you will find it with Allah."

Reflection: Prayer is an investment in our spiritual well-being and a way to seek closeness to Allah.

Prompt: How does this verse motivate you to view prayer as a form of self-improvement?

10. Surah Al-Ankabut (29:45)

"Indeed, prayer prohibits immorality and wrongdoing."

Reflection: Prayer purifies the soul, serving as a moral compass that keeps us on the right path.

Prompt: How has prayer helped you overcome personal challenges or bad habits?

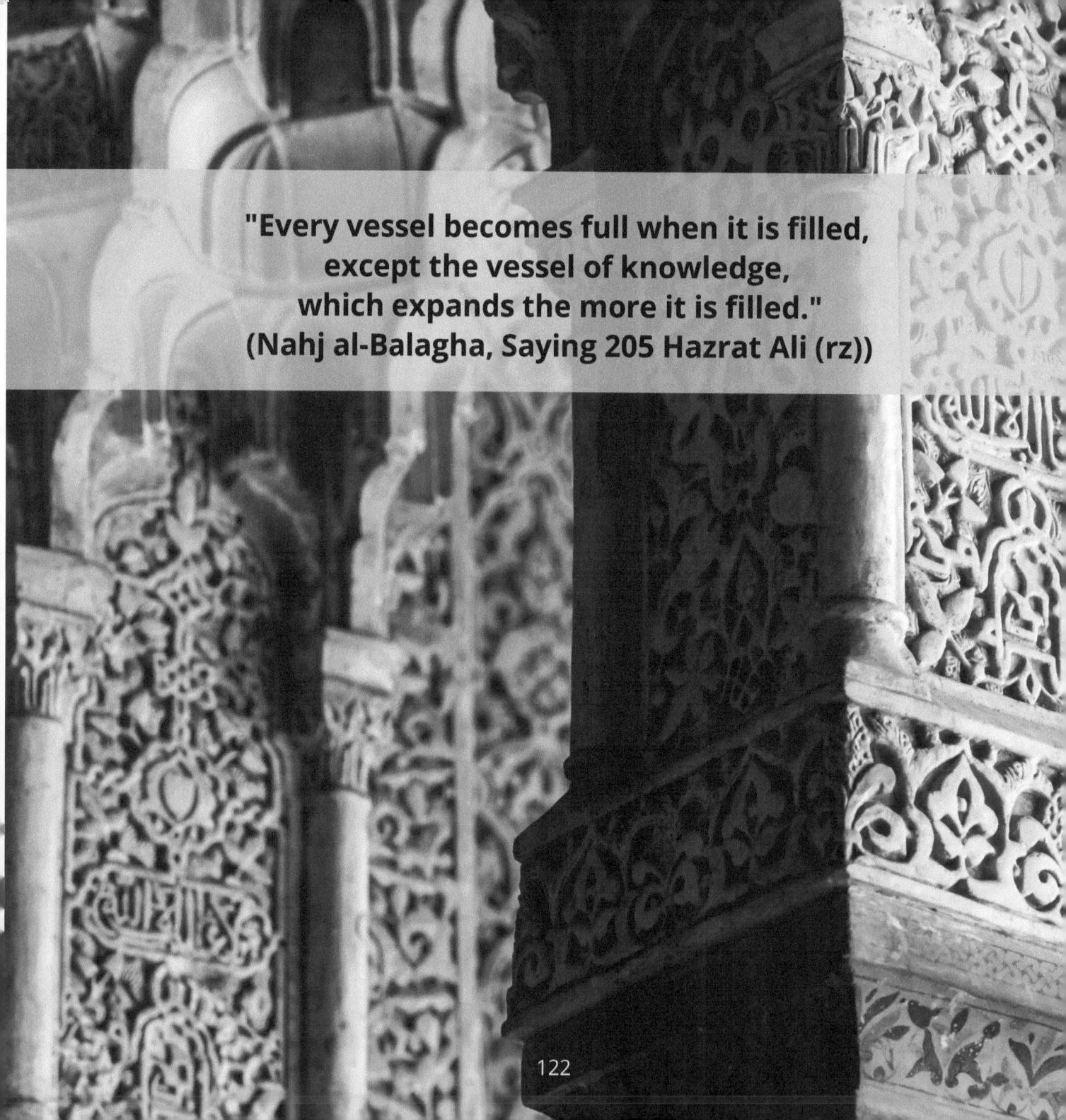

"Every vessel becomes full when it is filled,
except the vessel of knowledge,
which expands the more it is filled."
(Nahj al-Balagha, Saying 205 Hazrat Ali (rz))

"Look at what He created in the heavens and the earth; reflect on it, and you will see the signs of His greatness."
(Nahj al-Balagha, Sermon 182) Hazrat Ali (rz)

11. Surah Taha (20:14)

"Indeed, I am Allah. There is no deity except Me, so worship Me and establish prayer for My remembrance."

Reflection: Prayer is an act of devotion that strengthens our bond with Allah.

Prompt: How does prayer help you feel closer to Allah in your daily life?

12. Surah Al-Furqan (25:77)

"Say, 'What would my Lord care for you if not for your supplication?'"

Reflection: Our prayers matter to Allah, showing how much He values our connection with Him.

Prompt: How does this verse inspire you to make prayer a regular part of your day?

13. Surah Al-Imran (3:8)

"Our Lord, let not our hearts deviate after You have guided us and grant us from Yourself mercy. Indeed, You are the Bestower."

Reflection: Prayer helps protect our hearts from losing faith, keeping us aligned with Allah's guidance.

Prompt: How can you use this verse to remain steadfast in your faith?

14. Surah Al-A'raf (7:23)

"Our Lord, we have wronged ourselves, and if You do not forgive us and have mercy upon us, we will surely be among the losers."

Reflection: This heartfelt plea from Adam (AS) and Hawwa (AS) highlights the redemptive power of prayer.

Prompt: How does this verse inspire you to seek forgiveness through prayer?

15. Surah Ibrahim (14:40)

"My Lord, make me an establisher of prayer, and [many] from my descendants."

Reflection: This verse emphasizes the importance of prayer not just for ourselves, but for future generations.

Prompt: How can you inspire your family to value and establish prayer?

16. Surah Al-Anfal (8:33)
"But Allah would not punish them while they seek forgiveness."

Reflection: Prayer and repentance protect us from hardship and bring us closer to Allah's mercy.

Prompt: How does seeking forgiveness in prayer provide you with comfort and hope?

17. Surah Al-Kahf (18:10)

"Our Lord, grant us from Yourself mercy and prepare for us from our affair right guidance."

Reflection: The prayer of the companions of the cave shows how prayer brings clarity and guidance during uncertainty.

Prompt: How can this verse encourage you to pray for guidance in times of confusion?

18. Surah An-Nur (24:41)

"Do you not see that Allah is exalted by whoever is within the heavens and the earth and by the birds with wings spread [in flight]?"

Reflection: This verse shows that prayer and glorification of Allah are universal acts, connecting all of creation.

Prompt: How does reflecting on nature inspire your prayers?

19. Surah Al-Hajj (22:77)

"O you who have believed, bow and prostrate and worship your Lord and do good – that you may succeed."

Reflection: Success in life and faith is linked to worship, prayer, and doing good deeds.

Prompt: How can you balance prayer and action to achieve success?

20. Surah Al-Baqarah (2:201)

"Our Lord, give us in this world [that which is] good and in the Hereafter [that which is] good and protect us from the punishment of the Fire."

Reflection: This comprehensive prayer highlights the balance between worldly and spiritual well-being.

Prompt: How can you incorporate this dua into your daily routine for holistic blessings?

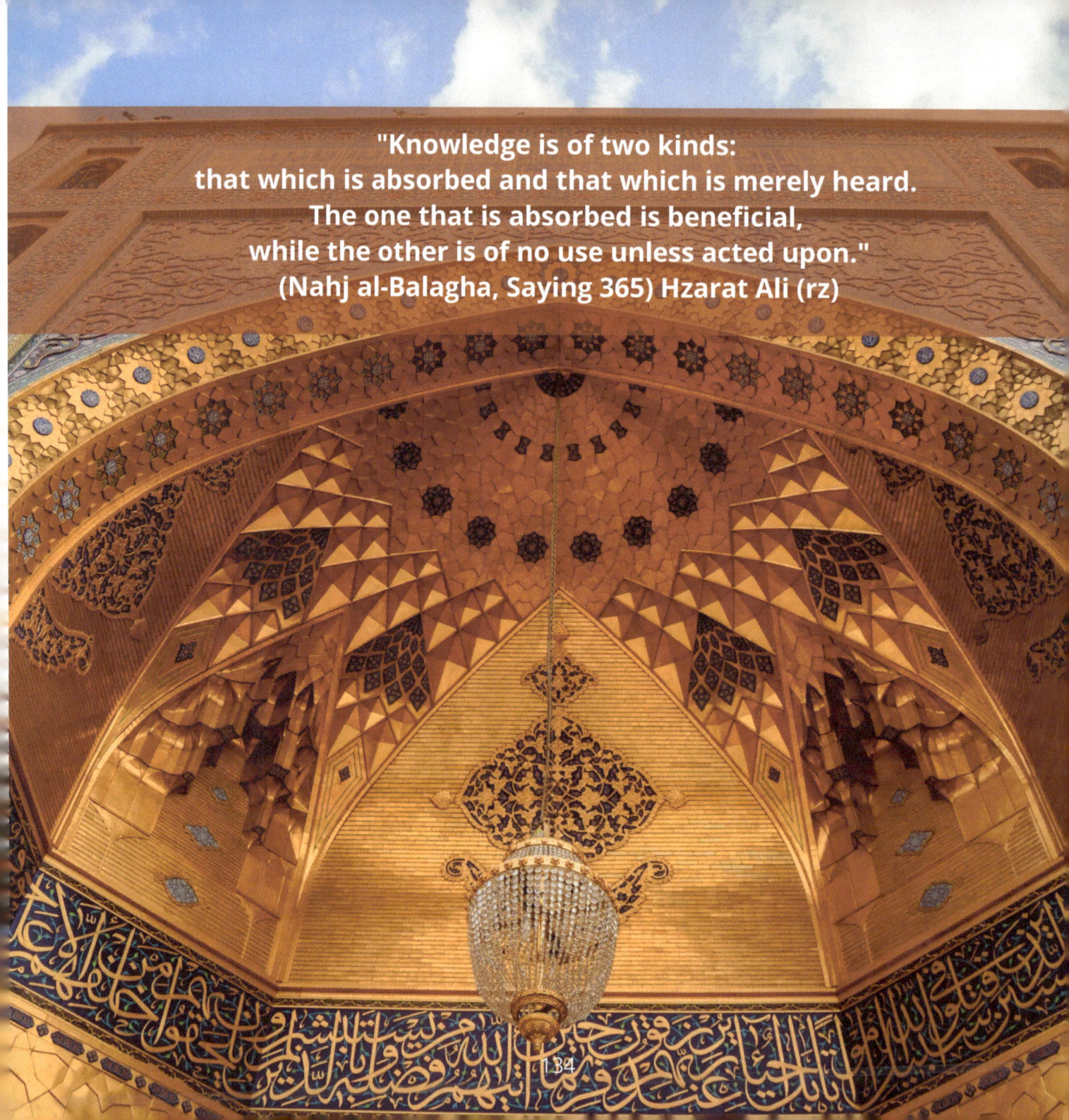

"Knowledge is of two kinds:
that which is absorbed and that which is merely heard.
The one that is absorbed is beneficial,
while the other is of no use unless acted upon."
(Nahj al-Balagha, Saying 365) Hzarat Ali (rz)

:

"Indeed, it is We (God) who sent down the Qur'an and indeed, We will be its guardian."

(Surah Al-Hijr 15:9)

" I pray that we all have the courage and sentiment to understand the true meaning of Quran, rather then just reciting it without any understanding of the true message.

I pray that we truley understand the meaning of this life that is in essence a Creator expecting love back from His creation and knowing it cannot be forced, creating this limited life with ups and downs to make us find moments of realisation of His Love and opportunity to connect back. All source of Love & Creation is only from One True God, Allah (sw)."

Ameen!

Muhammad
Sheraz Alvi

"Salamun Qolam Min Rabbi Rahim"
(Surah Ya-Sin 36:58)

"(And) "Peace," will be their greeting from The Merciful Lord".

Dont froget to get
Pearls of Quran Volume 2 & 3

Volume 2 focuses on:
- Miracles of Quran
- Contentment and Rida
- Sincerity in Worship
- Repentance to Allah
- Strength through Unity

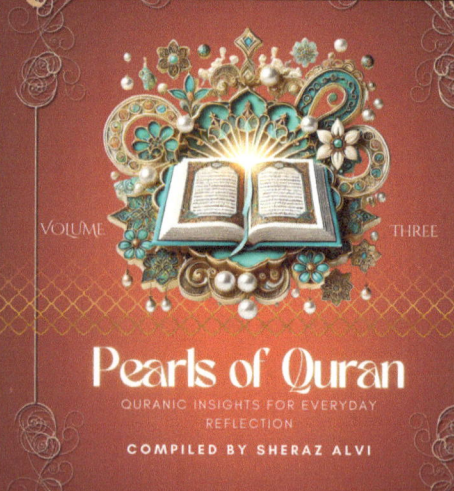

Volume 3 focuses on:
- The Value of Time
- Obedience to Parents
- The Role of Women in Islam
- Dignity and Self-Respect
- Health and Halal Living
- Environmental Stewardship